The Muslim Woman's and Muslim Man's Dress

According to the Qur'an and Sunnah

Compiled by Dr. Jamal A. Badawi

Ta-Ha Publishers Ltd.

Copyright © Ta-Ha Publishers Ltd. 1400AH/ 1980CE
First Published 1980
Reprinted in 1982, 1984, 1986, 1988, 1990, 1994, 1995, 1997, 1999
Revised in July 2006

Published by:
Ta-Ha Publishers Ltd.
1 Wynne Road
London SW9 0BB

Website: http://www.taha.co.uk
Email: sales@taha.co.uk

Written by: Dr. Jamal A. Badawi
General Editor: Dr. Abia Afsar-Siddiqui

A catalogue record of this book is available from the British Library.

ISBN: 1 842000 76 4

Printed and Bound in England by: De-Luxe Printers Ltd.

TABLE OF CONTENTS

يَـٰبَنِىٓ ءَادَمَ لَا يَفْتِنَنَّكُمُ ٱلشَّيْطَـٰنُ كَمَآ أَخْرَجَ أَبَوَيْكُم مِّنَ ٱلْجَنَّةِ يَنزِعُ عَنْهُمَا لِبَاسَهُمَا لِيُرِيَهُمَا سَوْءَٰتِهِمَآ

O Children of Adam! Let not the devil seduce you as he caused your (first) parents to go forth from the Garden and tore off from them their robe (of innocence) that he might manifest their shame to them...

(Surat Al-'Araf 7:27)

~ INTRODUCTION ~

To some, the subject of a Muslim's dress may sound trivial. The Shari'ah (Islamic Law), however, assigns it moral, social and legal dimensions.

At the very basic level, clothing serves to preserve modesty and protect from the elements. It can further be used to beautify, be a display of wealth and status or a means to identify one's belonging to a certain belief system or nationality. In addition, dress can also impact greatly on an individual's conduct and behaviour. Thus, the subject of dress is far from trivial.

Since Islam is a complete way of life, it inevitably contains detailed guidelines on the way in which both men and women should dress. These guidelines have been revealed by Allah and so our opinion on the subject should be subservient to whatever has been ordered by Allah and practised by the Prophet ﷺ.

وَمَا كَانَ لِمُؤْمِنٍ وَلَا مُؤْمِنَةٍ إِذَا قَضَى ٱللَّهُ وَرَسُولُهُ أَمْرًا أَن

يَكُونَ لَهُمُ ٱلْخِيَرَةُ مِنْ أَمْرِهِمْ وَمَن يَعْصِ ٱللَّهَ وَرَسُولَهُ فَقَدْ

ضَلَّ ضَلَلًا مُّبِينًا

It is not fitting for a believer, man or woman, when a matter has been decided by Allah and His Messenger, to have any option about their decision: if anyone disobeys Allah and His Messenger, he is indeed on a clearly wrong path.

(Surat Al-Ahzab 33:36)

Placing one's personal opinions, feelings or inclinations above or at the same level as the commandments of Allah is the ultimate in human pride and vanity. This means, in effect, that a mortal is responding to Allah's guidance by viewing it as Allah's opinion alone and believing that his own opinion is better for him than what his creator has revealed. [1]

Our faith is perfected only when we strive to follow all of the commands of Allah; we are not at liberty to choose the aspects of religion that fit into our lives. As the Qur'an states:

$$\text{أَفَتُؤْمِنُونَ بِبَعْضِ ٱلْكِتَبِ وَتَكْفُرُونَ بِبَعْضٍ}$$

...Then is it only a part of the Book that you believe in and do you reject the rest?...

(Surat Al-Baqarah 2:85)

This brief booklet presents the guidelines regarding the Muslim woman and Muslim man's dress according to the Qur'an and Sunnah. It is based on Muhammad Nasiruddin al-Albani's *Hijabul-Mar'at-il Muslimah fil Kitab Wassunnah*. Other sources of reference include the Qur'anic tafsirs of Ibn Kathir, Yusuf Ali and Sayyid Qutb; authorities in fiqh including Sayyid Sabiq's *Fiqh as-Sunnah* and Yusuf al-Qaradawi's *al-Halal wal-Haram fil-Islam*. (see Major References below)

---

1. A distinction should be made between: a) the acceptance of Allah's word as true and supreme in itself while not succeeding to implement it fully in one's life hoping and trying to reach that goal; and b) regarding one's own opinions or other social values and pressures as more valid than Allah's injunctions and trying to find various excuses to justify one's breaking of the laws of Allah. The latter is not only blameworthy but also akin to disbelief.

There are many other issues that could have been covered under the heading of this booklet, but are not mentioned here. The focus of this booklet is on the documented injunctions of Allah as derived from His Word (the Qur'an) and as explained by His Messenger, Muhammad ﷺ.

~ ~ ~ ~ ~ ~ ~ ~ ~ ~

MAJOR REFERENCES

Al-Qur'an - English translations of Yusuf Ali and M. Pickthall
Al-Hadith - as cited
Al-Albani, Muhammad N., *Hijabul-Mar'at-il Muslimah fil Kitab Wassunnah,* 3rd printing, Al-Maktab ul-Islami, Beirut (1969)
Al-Qaradawi, Yusuf, *al-Halal wal-Haram fil-Islam*, Maktabat Wahbah, Cairo (1976)
Sabiq, Sayyid, *Fiqh-as-Sunnah*, 2nd printing, Darul Kitab-il-Arabi, Beirut (1973)

~ ~ ~ ~ ~ ~ ~ ~ ~ ~

~ REQUIREMENTS OF A MUSLIM WOMAN'S DRESS ~

There are four basic requirements for the dress of a Muslim woman as outlined in the Qur'an and hadith. These are:

a) The extent of covering
b) Looseness of dress
c) Thickness of dress
d) Overall appearance

Additional requirements have been detailed in the hadith.

The First Requirement: Extent of Covering

The dress must cover the whole body except for the areas specifically exempted. The Qur'an states:

وَقُل لِّلْمُؤْمِنَـٰتِ يَغْضُضْنَ مِنْ أَبْصَـٰرِهِنَّ وَيَحْفَظْنَ فُرُوجَهُنَّ وَلَا

يُبْدِينَ زِينَتَهُنَّ إِلَّا مَا ظَهَرَ مِنْهَا وَلْيَضْرِبْنَ بِخُمُرِهِنَّ عَلَىٰ

جُيُوبِهِنَّ وَلَا يُبْدِينَ زِينَتَهُنَّ إِلَّا لِبُعُولَتِهِنَّ أَوْ ءَابَآئِهِنَّ

أَوْ ءَابَآءِ بُعُولَتِهِنَّ أَوْ أَبْنَآئِهِنَّ أَوْ أَبْنَآءِ بُعُولَتِهِنَّ أَوْ

إِخْوَٰنِهِنَّ أَوْ بَنِىٓ إِخْوَٰنِهِنَّ أَوْ بَنِىٓ أَخَوَٰتِهِنَّ أَوْ نِسَآئِهِنَّ أَوْ مَا

مَلَكَتْ أَيْمَـٰنُهُنَّ أَوِ ٱلتَّـٰبِعِينَ غَيْرِ أُوْلِى ٱلْإِرْبَةِ مِنَ ٱلرِّجَالِ أَوِ

ٱلطِّفْلِ ٱلَّذِينَ لَمْ يَظْهَرُوا عَلَىٰ عَوْرَٰتِ ٱلنِّسَآءِ وَلَا يَضْرِبْنَ

بِأَرْجُلِهِنَّ لِيُعْلَمَ مَا يُخْفِينَ مِن زِينَتِهِنَّ

And say to the believing women that they should lower their gaze and guard their modesty; that they should not display their beauty and ornaments except what (must ordinarily) appear thereof; that they should draw their veils over their bosoms and not display their beauty except to their husbands, their fathers, their husbands' fathers, their sons, their husbands' sons, their brothers or their brothers' sons or their sisters' sons, or their women, or the slaves whom their right hand possess or male servants free of physical needs, or small children who have no sense of the shame of sex; and that they should not strike their feet in order to draw attention to their hidden ornaments.

(Surat An-Nur 24:31)

This ayah contains, among other things, two main injunctions:

1. A Muslim woman should not display her beauty and adornment (*zeenah*) except for '*ma dhahara minha*' - 'that which must ordinarily appear of it'[2] or 'that which is apparent.'[3]

The word *zeenah*[4] lends itself to two related meanings:
i) natural or bodily beauty[5] and
ii) adornment such as rings, bracelets and clothes.

The part of *zeenah*, exempted from the above injunction by the words '*ma dhahara minha*', has been interpreted in two ways:

---

2. Abdullah Yusuf Ali, The Meaning of The Holy Qur'an
3. M. M. Pickthall, The Meaning of The Glorious Qur'an
4. According to *Lisan ul-'Arab* (Dictionary of Arabic Language), the term *zeenah* includes 'all that which beautifies', quoted in Ne'mat Sidqy, *At-Tabarruj*, 17th printing, Dar-ul-I'tisam, Egypt, 1975, pp. 20-21.
5. The term *zeenah* is used in the Qur'an to refer to children, wealth and natural beauty in Allah's creation. See, for example the following Qur'anic ayat: 17: 47, 16:8, 37:6 and 3:14.

i) The face and hands can be left uncovered. This is the interpretation of the majority of the jurists, past and present.[6] This interpretation is confirmed by *ijma'* (consensus) that a Muslim woman is allowed by Islam to uncover her face and hands during pilgrimage (Hajj and 'Umrah) and even during prayers (salah) while the rest of her body is regarded as *'awrah* (that which should be covered).[7] This interpretation is based on the authority of Prophet Muhammad ﷺ especially the hadith in which he states:

> '...If a woman reaches the age of puberty, no part of her body should be seen but this' - and he pointed to his face and hands.
>
> (Abu Dawud)

ii) That the whole body should be covered and *'ma dhahara minha'* refers to whatever appears of the woman's body owing to uncontrollable factors such as the blowing of wind or out of necessity such as bracelets or even the outer clothes themselves. One weakness with this stringent interpretation is that Allah does not hold one responsible for 'uncontrollable factors' and these are automatically forgiven without the need to specify this in the Qur'an. The fact that the Qur'an specifies a concession, means that there must be a concession over and above 'uncontrollable factors'. This is confirmed by the Abu Dawud hadith above.

2. The headcovers (*khumur*) should be drawn over the neck slits (*juyoob*). *Khumur* is the plural of the Arabic word *khimar* which

---

6. This is the interpretation of Malik, Ash-Shafi'i, Abu Hanifa and a version of Hanbal. See al-Albani pp. 41-42.

7. Al-Albani provides ample evidence that the covering of the face and hands is not required. Suffice to say that the woman is allowed to uncover her face and hands during such spiritual acts as pilgrimage (Hajj and 'Umrah) and prayer (salah). See al-Albani pp.25-26.

means a headcover.[8] *Juyoob* is the plural of the Arabic word *Jaiyb* (a derivative of *jawb* or cutting) and refers to the neck slit of the dress. This means that the headcover should be drawn so as to cover, not only the hair, but also the neck and the bosom.

The Second Requirement: Looseness of Dress

The dress must be loose enough so as not to decribe the shape of a woman's body. This is consistent with the intent of the ayah cited above (24:31) and is a crucial aspect of hiding *zeenah*. Even moderately tight clothes which cover the whole body do describe the shape of such attractive parts of the woman's body as the bustline, the waist, the buttocks, the back and the thighs. If these are not part of the natural beauty or *zeenah*, then what else is?

Prophet Muhammad ﷺ once received a thick garment as a gift. He gave it to Usamah bin Zayd ؓ who in turn gave it to his wife. When asked by the Prophet ﷺ why he did not wear it, Usamah indicated that he had given it to his wife. The Prophet then said to Usamah, 'Ask her to use a *gholalah* under it (the garment) for I fear that it (the garment) may describe the size of her bones.'[9] The word *gholalah* in Arabic means a thick fabric worn under the dress to prevent it from describing the shape of the body.[10]

---

8. This meaning of *khimar* was explained in such authorities as Ibn al-Atheer's *An-Nihaya* and *Tafseer-ul-Hafiz Ibn Kathir* and others. Al-Albani reports that he knows of no difference on this point. See al-Albani, pp. 33-34.
9. This hadith appears in Musnad Ahmad and al-Bayhaqi and is confirmed in other sources of hadith such as Sunan Abu Dawud. See al-Albani, pp. 59-63.
10. A thick garment may conceal the colour of the skin but not fully cover the shape of the body. Thus the Prophet ﷺ suggested the use of a *gholalah*. See al-Albani, p.60.

A highly desirable way of concealing the shape of the body is to wear a cloak over the garment. The Prophet ﷺ however indicated that if the woman's dress meets the Islamic standards it suffices (without a cloak) even for the validity of prayers.[11]

The Third Requirement: Thickness of Dress

The dress should be thick enough so as not to show the colour of the skin it covers or the shape of the body which it is supposed to hide.

The purpose of ayah (24:31) is to hide the Muslim woman's body except *ma dhahara minha* (the face and hands). It is obvious that this purpose cannot be served if the dress is thin enough to reveal the colour of the skin or the shape or beauty of the body. This is eloquently explained by the Prophet Muhammad ﷺ:

'In later (generations) of my Ummah there will be women who will be dressed but naked. On top of their heads (what looks) like camel humps. Curse them for they are truly cursed.' In another version he added that they 'will not enter paradise or (even) get a smell of it.'[12]

(At-Tabari and Muslim)

On one occasion, Asma ؓ (daughter of Abu Bakr Siddiq ؓ) was visiting her sister Aishah ؓ (wife of the Prophet ﷺ). When the Prophet ﷺ noticed that Asma's dress was not thick enough he turned his face away in anger and said:

---

11. See Sayyid Sabiq's *Fiqh-as-Sunnah*, p. 127.
12. See al-Albani p.56.

'If a woman reaches the age of puberty, no part of her body should be seen, but this, and he pointed to his face and hands.'[13]

(Abu Dawud)

The Fourth Requirement: Overall Appearance

The Muslim woman's dress should not be such that it attracts men's attention to the woman's beauty. The Qur'an clearly prescribes the requirements of the woman's dress for the purpose of concealing *zeenah* (adornment). How can *zeenah* be concealed if the dress is designed in such a way that it attracts men's eyes to the woman?

This is why the Qur'an, addressing the Prophet's wives as examples for Muslim women, says:

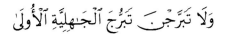

Bedizen not yourselves with the bedizenment of the Time of Ignorance...[14]

(Surat Al-Ahzab 33:33)

---

13. On another occasion when the Prophet ﷺ saw a bride in a thin dress, he said, "She is not a woman who believes in Surat an-Nur who wears this." This is the surah in which the main requirements of the Muslim woman's dress are outlined. On another occasion, some women from the tribe of Bani Tameem came to visit Aishah ﴾ in thin clothes. Upon seeing them, the Prophet ﷺ said, "If you are believers, then these are not the clothes of believers." See Yusuf al-Qaradawi p. 160.

14. The term used in the Qur'an is *tabarruj*, which means displaying of beauty. Another derivative of *tabarruj* is *burooj*, which is used in the Qur'an (e.g. 4:77, 15:16, 25:61, 85:1). *Burooj* means tower implying clear visibility. Clear visibility of a woman may result from her type of dress, the way she walks or the way she behaves.

Additional Requirements [15]

In addition to the above four main and clearly spelled out requirements, there are other requirements whose specific applications may vary with time and location. These include:

1. The dress should not be similar to what is known as a male costume. Ibn Abbas narrated that:

> 'The Prophet cursed the men who act like women and the women who act like men.'[16]
>
> (Al-Bukhari, Abu Dawud, Ahmad and Ad-Darimi)

2. It should not be similar to what is known as the dress of the unbelievers. This requirement is derived from the general rule of Shariah that Muslims should have their distinct personality and differentiate their practice and appearance from unbelievers.[17]

3. It should not be a dress of fame, pride and vanity. Such fame may be sought by wearing an excessively fancy dress as a status symbol or an excessively ragged dress to gain admiration of one's selflessness. Both motives are improper by Islamic standards. The Prophet ﷺ says that:

> 'Whoever wears a dress of fame in this world, Allah will clothe him with a dress of humiliation on the day of resurrection then set it afire.'[18]
>
> (Abu Dawud)

---

15. According to al-Albani, a further requirement is that the dress should not be perfumed. In fact, this requirement extends beyond dress.There are several ahadith which make it clearly forbidden for a Muslim woman to wear perfume when she leaves her house, even to go to the mosque. See al-Albani, pp. 64-66.
16. For this and other ahadith on the subject see al-Albani, pp. 66-69.
17. See al-Albani pp.78-109.
18. For this and other versions of the hadith, see al-Albani pp.110-111.

~ REQUIREMENTS OF A MUSLIM MAN'S DRESS ~

قُل لِّلْمُؤْمِنِينَ يَغُضُّوا مِنْ أَبْصَرِهِمْ وَيَحْفَظُوا فُرُوجَهُمْ

ذَٰلِكَ أَزْكَىٰ لَهُمْ إِنَّ ٱللَّهَ خَبِيرٌ بِمَا يَصْنَعُونَ

Say to the believing men that they should lower their gaze
and guard their modesty; that will make for greater purity
for them. And Allah is well acquainted with all that they do.
(Surat An-Nur 24:30)

It should be noted that the basic requirements of the Muslim woman's dress apply as well to Muslim man's clothing with the difference being mainly in degree. This can best be understood by looking into what Islam defines as *'awrah* which refers to the part of the body that should be covered at all times unless there is an expressed exception. The covering of *'awrah* is also a condition for the validity of prayers for both men and women. While the *'awrah* for the woman is defined as the whole body except for the face and hands, for the man the *'awrah* is defined as the area between the navel and the knees.[19]

Within the definition of *'awrah* for men and women, all the four basic requirements discussed in this paper are essentially the same:

1. The man should fully cover his *'awrah*.

---

19. Difference exists among jurists as to whether the knees and the thighs should be included in the definition of a man's *'awrah*. For a good discussion on the evidence related to both views, see Sayyid Sabiq's *Fiqh as-Sunnah*, vol. 1, pp.125-127.

2. His *'awrah* should be covered in a loose garment so as not to describe the part that should be covered.

3. The garment should be thick enough so as not to describe the colour of the skin or the parts required to be covered.

4. The dress should not be designed in a way to attract attention. The basic rules of modesty and avoiding 'show off' applies to all believing men and women.

The three other additional requirements discussed under the Muslim woman's code of dress apply to men's clothes as well.

1. They should not be similar to what is known as the female dress.

2. They should not be similar to what could be identified as the dress of unbelievers.

3. They should not be clothes of fame, pride and vanity.

There is one further restriction specific to men's apparel only:

> The Prophet ﷺ took some silk in his right hand and some gold in his left, declaring, "These two are haram for the males among my followers, but halal for females."
>
> (Ibn Majah)

~ ~ ~ ~ ~ ~ ~ ~ ~